I Know God Is Real

This book is for everyone in the whole world.

- Ethan Trory Taylor

To: constance
From: Ethan Taylor

Hi, my name is Ethan Taylor and I have something very important to tell you.

It is something that everyone in the whole world needs to know.

Some people think that God is a legend.

They think he is a story for children.

Some people even think he is a lie.

I want to tell you that God is real.

Every time I wake up,

I know God is Real.

I thank God for waking me up,

I know I can not wake myself up.

Every time I see the sun,

I know
God is real.

I thank God
for making the Sun.

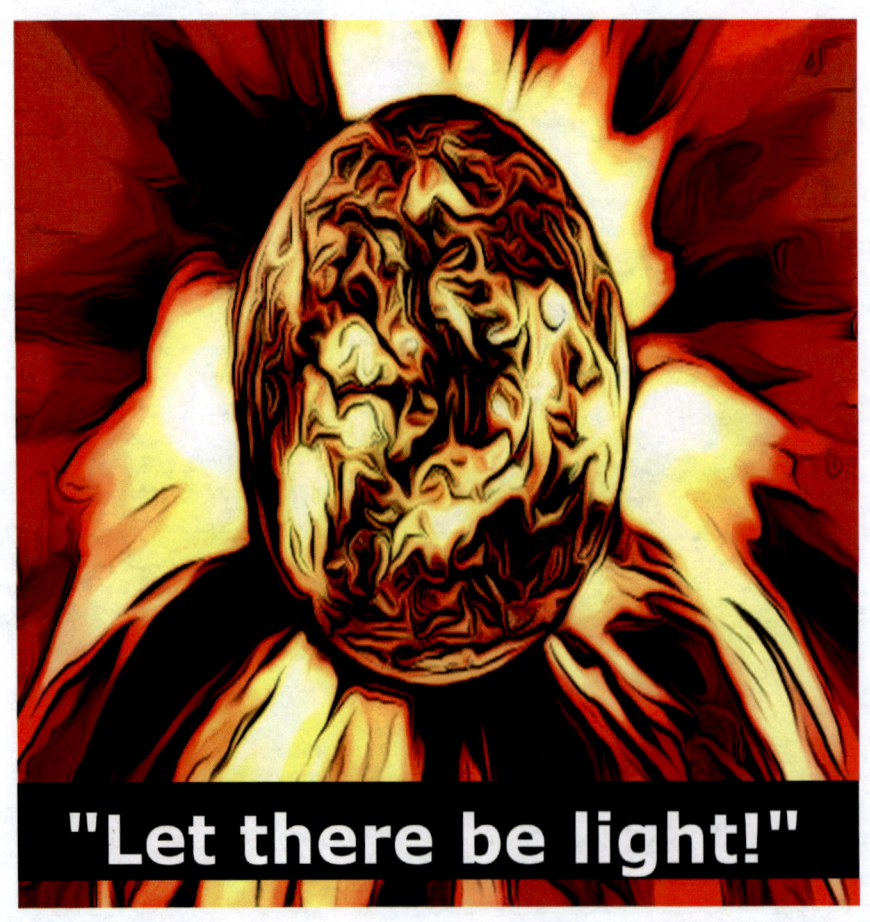

"Let there be light!"

It helps us to stay warm.

Every time I see plants,

I know God is real.

I thank
God for plants.

They help us to breathe.

Every time I see a rainbow,

I know
God is real.

I thank God because he promised to

never destroy the earth with water again.

Every time I see my house,

I know God is real.

I thank God for giving us a place to live.

We prayed and he blessed my mom and me with a house.

So never forget

God is real.

The End.